PRAYING

FOR DIVINE

BLESSINGS

... OH LORD, BLESS ME INDEED

JOE-JESIMIEL OGBE

Praying For Divine Blessings

Copyright- 2018 Joe Jesimiel Ogbe

ISBN - 978-978-55429-1-2

Published in Nigeria by:

Young Disciples Press

For Further information or permission, contact:

Director of Publication

Young Disciples International (YDI)

3, YDI Street,

Off Isheri- Lasu Express Road,

By Soulos Hotel Bus-Stop,

Igando, Lagos Nigeria

Tel. 08023124455, 08033475807, 01-2934286

Contents

Dedication.. v

Introduction.. 1

Chapter One... 9

THE PRAYER-ANSWERING GOD

Chapter Two.. 19

PRAYING FOR SPIRITUAL BLESSINGS

Chapter Three... 25

PRAYING FOR ABRAHAMIC BLESSINGS

Chapter Four 33

PRAYING FOR MATERIAL BLESSINGS

Chapter Five 39

PRAYING FOR FINANCIAL BLESSINGS

Chapter Six 47

PRAYING FOR SUNDRY BLESSINGS

Chapter Seven... 55

PRAYING FOR FAVOUR

Chapter Eight 63

PRAYING FOR SOCIAL BLESSINGS

Chapter Nine 71

PRAYING FOR HEALTH AND HEALING

Chapter Ten.. 77

PRAYING AGAINST SATANIC FORCES

Epilogue.. 83

PRAYING FOR OTHER PEOPLE

Other Books by the Author 91

Dedication

To the believer who is bereft of tangible blessings. This book is my humble attempt to help you navigate your way into the blessings of God.

Introduction

My dear reader, may I sincerely appreciate you for picking up this prayer manual to peruse its pages. By this wise and noble action, you are making a clear statement that you are interested in partaking in the blessings of God. Let me assure you that you will not be disappointed, as God has assured me that everyone who reads this book in faith and prays accordingly will be blessed indeed in the order of Jabez.

The truth is that you can never be anything worthwhile in this life outside of the blessings of God. Experiencing a perennial "lack of blessings" will make you miss out on your destiny or true callings in life. If you don't want to be a "nobody" or nonentity in the journey of life, you must decide now to pray your way into blessings indeed.

This book is my modest attempt to help you provoke terrific testimony of blessings via heartfelt prayers !

This year 2018 marks the 40th anniversary of my New Life in Christ Jesus, as I got born again in 1978. Over these years, I can eminently testify of God's blessings in my life.

God Almighty, my Heavenly Father, has blessed me beyond measure, description and comprehension! For instance, He has blessed me spiritually via the finished work of Jesus Christ on the cross of Calvary. In Christ, I am blessed. That means I'm superlatively and supremely favoured by God. He has declared good things about me or pronounced good things for my benefits and destiny. The good things that God has decreed for me are beyond my asking or imagination. Apostle Paul validates my assertion in this passage: *"Now unto him that is able to do exceeding abundantly above all that we ask or think, according to the power that worketh in us."*

Ephesians 3:20

Honestly, I can confirm that some of the blessings I have been enjoying, I did not bargain for or asked for them, while some came simply because I cried for them like Jabez. The Bible says, *"And Jabez called on the God of Israel, saying, Oh that thou wouldest bless me indeed, and enlarge my coast, and that thine hand might be with me, and that thou wouldest keep me from evil, that it may not grieve me! And God granted him that which he requested."*

1 Chronicles 4:10

Jabez prayed vehemently for blessings, and he was not disappointed, as God answered all his prayer requests. Many of us, like Jabez, are desperate to experience blessings. We even talk about it excitedly, and long to pray

2

for a blessing, but do we really know what a blessing is all about?

A blessing is the invocation of a thing conducive to happiness or welfare. When God called father Abraham to go to the Promised Land, He promised to bless him, make his name great, and through him, to bless all the families of the earth. The blessings here are plainly associated with happiness and welfare, both for Abraham and others.

A Blessing is also a God-given power or endowment for us to do that which we are designed and fabricated to do. For instance, we were supposed to fill the earth and multiply – so God gave us His blessing. That is, His ability or power to do it.

In a nutshell, a blessing is about God granting the power to do what He wants us and intends us to do. A blessing is a very positive thing! There is nothing negative about it!

There are blessings and there are blessings! Not all blessings are blessings indeed. For instance, a gift of fifty thousand Naira is a blessing, but a gift of fifty million Naira is a blessing indeed. A gift of salvation is a blessing indeed because its value or worth is superior to any material or financial blessing.

Why Do We Need Blessings?

Myles Munroe, of blessed memory, said, **"If purpose is not known, abuse is inevitable."** There is a purpose for the blessings of God. There is a reason God has unleashed His blessings on us! Having an understanding of the purpose of blessings will make you engage or use the blessings in the right way that will bring glory to God. Don't be like some people who want the blessing to show off. Rather seek the blessings so that you may become a channel of blessing to others. Seek God's blessings to fulfill His original design for your creation. You and I are designed to experience prosperity, peace, and fulfillment, but that design was ruined when sin entered the world. But thanks be to God who has graciously given humanity the ultimate blessing of salvation. The blessing of forgiveness that comes through faith in Jesus Christ cannot be measured or quantified by any earthly standard. The earthly, material, financial blessings we enjoy from day to day are temporary, but the spiritual blessings available to us in Christ encompasses time and eternity.

How Do We Access The Blessings?

Fundamentally, we access the Blessings via our acceptance of Jesus Christ as our Lord and saviour. The Bible says, *"But as many as received him, to them gave he power to become the sons of God, even to them that believe on his name .Which were born, not of blood, nor of the will of the flesh, nor of the will of man, but of God."*

John 1:12-13

Our new life in Christ or born again status guarantees our blessings. But we also need to take personal responsibility by asking for them in heartfelt and faith-filled prayers. The Bible says, *"And I say unto you, Ask, and it shall be given you; seek, and ye shall find; knock, and it shall be opened unto you. For every one that asketh receiveth; and he that seeketh findeth; and to him that knocketh it shall be opened."*

Luke 11:9-10

Jacob as a covenant child of God was blessed because he desperately prayed that he be blessed by the angel of God. The Bible says, *"And he said, Let me go, for the day breaketh. And he said, I will not let thee go, except thou bless me. And he said unto him, What is thy name? And he said, Jacob. And he said, Thy name shall be called no more Jacob, but Israel: for as a prince hast thou power with God and with men, and hast prevailed."*

Genesis 32:26-28

Jacob and Jabez are my two major biblical characters who prayed desperately for divine blessings and they were not disappointed as their prayers were answered. You too can travail in prayers for any type of blessing of your choice, and you shall not be disappointed.

Praying With The Word

The Word of God remains our incontrovertible authority. The Word is replete with all manner of blessings. Whatever blessing you are looking for can be found or located in the Word. Hence, the need to pray with the Word. The Bible says, *"For as the rain cometh down, and the snow from heaven, and returneth not thither, but watereth the earth, and maketh it bring forth and bud, that it may give seed to the sower, and bread to the eater: So shall my word be that goeth forth out of my mouth: it shall not return unto me void, but it shall accomplish that which I please, and it shall prosper in the thing whereto I sent it."*

Isaiah 55:10-11

In the above passage, God's Word is likened to the rain that pours down from heaven. It is loaded with blessings of all kinds, shapes and sizes. If you locate and receive the Word in faith and move further to pray with it, you will experience blessings of your choice. God has promised that His Word will not return to Him void, that is, His Word would not fail to deliver results, in our context - blessings.

Peter said, "... *Master we have toiled all the night and have taken nothing, nevertheless at thy Word I will let down the net"* Luke 5:5

Peter and co wanted a fruitful labour but they got frustration instead. The "sent or right word" from the lips of Jesus ended their frustration and fruitlessness! When you and I decree what we want, based on the authority, efficacy and integrity of the Word, we shall surely trigger the blessings packaged in the Word.

Do you want to be blessed beyond measure all the days of your life?

Do you want your family members to become true examples of divine blessings?

Do you want the work of your hands or business to command blessings?

Then be prepared and willing to pray according to the Word of God, which is the will of God!

A "Blessing indeed" is the will of God for you!

God is not a respecter of persons. What He did for others, He will do much more for you. Only be willing and prepared to pray with desperation like Jacob and Jabez.

Joe Jesimiel Ogbe

joejesimiel2006@yahoo.com

October, 2018.

Chapter One

THE PRAYER-ANSWERING GOD

God is still in the business of answering prayers today. God does not store prayers. He loves to answer them. But is God under any obligation to answer or say "yes" to every prayer? Not at all! He cannot answer any prayer that is antithetical to His will. He only answers prayers that align with His sovereign will. The Bible says, *"And this is the confidence that we have in him, that, if we ask any thing according to his will, he heareth us: 15 And if we know that he hear us, whatsoever we ask, we know that we have the petitions that we desired of him."*

1 John 5:14-15

How Do I Know God Will Answer Your Prayers?

Firstly, the Bible says, *"God is not a man, that he should lie; neither the son of man, that he should repent: hath he said, and shall he not do it? or hath he spoken, and shall he not make it good?"*

Numbers 23:19

God is not given to lies or deception! He does what He promises! He makes good His word. He cannot promise and fail. As such, His ever abiding faithfulness to promises gives me the confidence that He will answer you when you call upon Him. Check out these scriptures:

"He shall call upon me, and I will answer him: I will be with him in trouble; I will deliver him, and honour him."

Psalms 91:15

"Then shall ye call upon me, and ye shall go and pray unto me, and I will hearken unto you."

Jeremiah 29:12

"Call unto me, and I will answer thee, and shew thee great and mighty things, which thou knowest not."

Jeremiah 33:3

Secondly, God's dealings with others give credence to my position that He will answer you, if your faith is in proper alignment. Are there records in the scriptures when God answered people who trusted Him? If yes, then be rest assured that your case shall not be different. Have the assurance that He will answer you too. After all, He is not a respecter of persons! What He did for one, He will do for another! *"Then Peter opened his mouth, and said, Of a truth I perceive that God is no respecter of persons: But in every nation he that feareth him, and worketh righteousness, is accepted with him."*

Acts 10:34-35

12 Biblical Examples of Answered Prayers:

### 1.	God answered Abraham's servant's prayer for good speed

"And he said, O LORD God of my master Abraham, I pray thee, send me good speed this day, and shew kindness unto my master Abraham.

Behold, I stand here by the well of water; and the daughters of the men of the city come out to draw water: And let it come to pass, that the damsel to whom I shall say, Let down thy pitcher, I pray thee, that I may drink; and she shall say, Drink, and I will give thy camels drink also: let the same be she that thou hast appointed for thy servant Isaac; and thereby shall I know that thou hast shewed kindness unto my master. And it came to pass, before he had done speaking, that, behold, Rebekah came out, who was born to Bethuel, son of Milcah, the wife of Nahor, Abraham's brother, with her pitcher upon her shoulder."

Genesis 24:12-15

2. God answered Jacob's prayer for deliverance from the hand of Esau, his brother, as He granted him grace in the sight of Esau.

"Deliver me, I pray thee, from the hand of my brother, from the hand of Esau: for I fear him, lest he will come and smite me, and the mother with the children."

Genesis 32:11

"And Jacob said, Nay, I pray thee, if now I have found grace in thy sight, then receive my present at my hand: for therefore I have seen thy face, as though I had seen the face of God, and thou wast pleased with me. Take, I pray thee, my blessing that is brought to thee; because God hath dealt graciously with me, and because I have enough. And he urged him, and he took it."

Genesis 33:10-11

3. God answered Ezra and co when they prayed and fasted for protection

"For I was ashamed to require of the king a band of soldiers and horsemen to help us against the enemy in the way: because we had spoken unto the king, saying, The hand of our God is upon all them for good that seek him; but his power and his wrath is against all them that forsake him. So we fasted and besought our God for this: and he was intreated of us."

Ezra 8:22-23

4. God answered Samson's prayer for strength to avenge his two eyes that were plucked off by the Philistines

"And Samson called unto the LORD, and said, O Lord GOD, remember me, I pray thee, and strengthen me, I pray thee, only this once, O God, that I may be at once avenged of the Philistines for my two eyes."

Judges 16:28

5. God answered Samuel's request for thunder and rain.

"So Samuel called unto the LORD; and the LORD sent thunder and rain that day: and all the people greatly feared the LORD and Samuel."

1 Samuel 12:18

6. God answered Hannah's prayer for a son.

"Wherefore it came to pass, when the time was come about after Hannah had conceived, that she bare a son, and called his name Samuel, saying, Because I have asked him of the LORD."

1 Samuel 1:20

7.   God answered Isaac's prayer for his wife.

"And Isaac intreated the LORD for his wife, because she was barren: and the LORD was intreated of him, and Rebekah his wife conceived."

Genesis 25:21

8.   God answered Hezekiah's prayer.

"Then Hezekiah turned his face toward the wall, and prayed unto the LORD, And said, Remember now, O LORD, I beseech thee, how I have walked before thee in truth and with a perfect heart, and have done that which is good in thy sight. And Hezekiah wept sore. Then came the word of the LORD to Isaiah, saying, Go, and say to Hezekiah, Thus saith the LORD, the God of David thy father, I have heard thy prayer, I have seen thy tears: behold, I will add unto thy days fifteen years."

Isaiah 38:2-5

9.   God answered David when he called on Him in distress.

"I called upon the LORD in distress: the LORD answered me, and set me in a large place."

Psalms 118:5

10.   God answered Jabez's prayer for blessing, enlargement and preservation.

"And Jabez called on the God of Israel, saying, Oh that thou wouldest bless me indeed, and enlarge my coast, and that thine hand might be with me, and that thou wouldest keep me from evil, that it may not grieve me! And God granted him that which he requested."

1 Chronicles 4:10

11.   God answered Manasseh's Supplications.

"And when he was in affliction, he besought the LORD his God, and humbled himself greatly before the God of his fathers, And prayed unto him: and he was intreated of him, and heard his supplication, and brought him again to Jerusalem into his kingdom. Then Manasseh knew that the LORD he was God."

2Chro 33:12-13

12.   The Lord heard a Poor Man's Cry.

"This poor man cried, and the LORD heard him, and saved him out of all his troubles."

Psalms 34:6

My Personal Testimonies of Answered Prayers.

I also have a catalogue of testimonies of answered prayers but space will not allow me to share all. But let me in a jiffy share just two testimonies with you:

1.   Fruit of the womb

After our wedding in 1990, my wife and I wanted to have children but to no avail. We waited for nearly five years before God put to shame the wishes of evil people. Even one of my aunties who was known as a witch had declared that I was not going to have children because of her hatred for my mother. We visited many gynaecologists and their reports were not palatable to us. Having rejected their negative reports, we resorted to walking by faith and prayers. Then the God of answers showed up on our behalf and blessed us with the fruit of the womb. Today, we are blessed with three lovely young men to the glory of God. To get the full gist of our testimony of how we worked in faith, please read my book, "Getting what you want by Faith."

2.   Financial Supplies

As a minister, I have learnt over the years to depend on God for our supplies, both material and financial. Early in the ministry, I came across George Muller's book, where he shared copiously testimonies of how the needs of his orphanage were met miraculously by God. He had resolved not to ask man for the needs of his ministry but to look up to God alone. I loved his testimonies and decided that I too would never go cap in hand begging any man for my ministry needs. To God alone be all the glory, as He has become our faithful Source and Provider from inception till date. To us in Ydi, Greathouse Mandate church and WittyClass Academy, prayer has become a major key which we engage regularly to secure divine answers and intervention.

For instance, one day, we needed much money for our building construction as there was nothing on ground, so I quickly mobilised some of my youth leaders in YDI to engage in a heartfelt prayer, calling on God to stir up the hearts of our partners to remember us. The faithful God showed up immediately by moving a partner to give a large amount of money to YDI. The beloved partner said she was led to sow the financial seed because she was instructed to do so via revelation she received from the Lord.

Glory to God! My great God is still in the business of answering prayers today! And you're the next in line! Believe Him!

Chapter Two
PRAYING FOR
SPIRITUAL BLESSINGS

"Blessed be the God and Father of our Lord Jesus Christ, who hath blessed us with all spiritual blessings in heavenly places in Christ: According as he hath chosen us in him before the foundation of the world, that we should be holy and without blame before him in love: Having predestinated us unto the adoption of children by Jesus Christ to himself, according to the good pleasure of his will,"

Ephesians 1:3-5

B efore you start praying for or taking delivery of the spiritual blessings, you must first come to the sound knowledge and understanding of what a spiritual blessing is all about.

Spiritual blessings are those divine blessings which God has graciously given to us through the finished work of

Jesus Christ on the cross of Calvary. In Christ, you and I are blessed. That means we are superlatively and supremely favoured by God. In Christ, we are completely satisfied as God has packaged all we need in Him. In Christ Jesus there is no lack. In Him, we can say eminently and confidently that God has designed and fabricated good things for us. The truth is that the good things that God has decreed for us are probably beyond our ability to number.

Spiritual blessings are also spiritual gifts which God has bestowed on us so we can help one another. The Bible says, *"To one person the Spirit gives the ability to give wise advice; to another the same Spirit gives a message of special knowledge. The same Spirit gives great faith to another, and to someone else the one Spirit gives the gift of healing. He gives one person the power to perform miracles, and another the ability to prophesy. He gives someone else the ability to discern whether a message is from the Spirit of God or from another spirit. Still another person is given the ability to speak in unknown languages, while another is given the ability to interpret what is being said. It is the one and only Spirit who distributes all these gifts. He alone decides which gift each person should have."* - 1 Corinthians 12:7-11 (NLT).

The spiritual blessings are the blessings that the physical blessings are connected to. All things are first spiritual. The spiritual realm is more real than the physical realm. Someone said, "God planted the garden of Eden. The seed came from Heaven. The earth was to be replica or copy of Heaven."

The Heavenly realm is blessed with no sickness but health. No poverty but prosperity. No depression but joy. No anxiety but peace. These are the spiritual blessings available to us in Heavenly places. Go get yours today!

Prayer of Faith is required as the conduit to bring or manifest the spiritual blessings into the physical world. With prayers you can call forth the spiritual blessings from Heaven to manifest the physical blessings by using the name of Jesus. In your prayers you can call the spiritual blessings that God has already provided to impact and change the physical realm you live in. The truth is that many of us are yet to call forth all that God has made available in the spiritual realm. It's like you have money in the bank but you are starved of funds simply because you fail to ask for it.

What a tragedy!

PRAYERS:

1.   Father God, in the name of Jesus Christ I humbly come to you confessing my sins and iniquities. I earnestly seek and ask for your forgiveness. I believe that Christ died to take my punishment and that He has now given me a new life. Father God, may I enjoy all the blessings that accompany salvation which Christ has secured for me. Help me O Lord, to always long to constantly seek and

savour the spiritual blessings available to me in Christ Jesus which encompasses time and eternity. Help me by your grace to earnestly prioritise spiritual blessings above other types of blessings.

2.   Father God, now that I have become your child via Jesus Christ, kindly place your mark of ownership on me, guaranteeing my eternal security in Christ. I receive spiritual blessing to co-labour with You as a Christ ambassador bringing the message of reconciliation to humanity. And may the peace that passes all understanding and the assurance that nothing is able to separate me from your love that is in Christ Jesus keep me steadfast in Christ forever.

3.   Father God, by faith I know that you have chosen me in Christ before the foundation of the world, that I should be holy and without blame before you in love. Heavenly Father, what a joy to know that you have decided to make me holy and blameless, as a result of your abiding love, good pleasure and grace.

4.   Quicken me, O God for your name's sake and for your righteousness' sake, bring my soul out of spiritual dryness. Father God, let every spiritual dryness in my life and family come to an end right now in Jesus mighty name. Deliver me, O Lord from spiritual barrenness.

5.   Father God, in the name of Jesus Christ, let me have a burning desire always to see and experience your showers of spiritual blessings. Oh God, cause me to flourish spiritually like a palm tree and grow up like cedar in Lebanon.

6.   Father God, your will for me is that the dry places of my life become as a well-watered garden, put within me the ability to be fat and flourishing spiritually in Jesus name.

7.   Father God, I know that if there is no thirst, there is no access to your blessings. Today, I ask for grace to yearn desperately for the release of spiritual blessings.

8.   Father God, in the name of Jesus Christ, create in me a genuine thirst for righteousness. Today, by your power, I receive grace to hunger and thirst for righteousness.

9.   Father God, in the name of Jesus Christ, help me to develop the passion and discipline to seek you early like David. Father God, create in me a new heart that will always and constantly crave for you and your kingdom.

10.   Father God, in the name of Jesus Christ, as I desire the release and outpouring of the rain of the Spirit, arise and bless me with the gifts of the Spirit so I can serve your purpose.

Chapter Three

PRAYING FOR
ABRAHAMIC BLESSINGS

The Bible says, "A faithful man shall abound with blessings..."

Abraham was a faithful man in the scriptures that amassed great blessings. He was so blessed of the Lord that he became a channel of blessing to all the families of the earth. The truth is that the Abrahamic blessings are real, and these blessings could be yours if you desire and appropriate them into your life via a veritable relationship with Jesus Christ. The Bible says, *"That the blessing of Abraham might come on the Gentiles through Jesus Christ; that we might receive the promise of the Spirit through faith."*

Galatians 3:14

Abraham was not just a friend of another man but a friend of God! Do you know what it means to be called a friend of an influential man? It means you have privileges that non-friends would never have.

"But thou, Israel, art my servant, Jacob whom I have chosen, the seed of Abraham my friend."

Isaiah 41:8

One of the privileges of friendship is that your friend will answer you when you call upon him.

Please note that through Abraham's friendship with God, we too have become friends of God, just as we are sons of God via Jesus Christ, the Son of God!

Are you of faith? *If yes, then you are a child of Abraham! "Know ye therefore that they which are of faith, the same are the children of Abraham."*

Galatians 3:7

If you are of faith, I mean if you relate to God on the basis of faith, you too are blessed in the order of Abraham. The Bible says, *"So then they which be of faith are blessed with faithful Abraham."*

Galatians 3:9

The Bible says, *"And if ye be Christ's, then are ye Abraham's seed, and heirs according to the promise."* Galatians 3:29

Do you belong to Jesus Christ? Then you are Abraham's seed like Isaac and Jacob. As a seed, you have the authority, boldness or courage to call upon God confidently, and you will get a favourable answer! "Let us therefore come boldly unto the throne of grace, that we may obtain mercy, and find grace to help in time of need." Hebrew 4:16

Covet the Abrahamic blessings and pray accordingly:

1. Change of name

"Neither shall thy name any more be called Abram, but thy name shall be Abraham; for a father of many nations have I made thee."

Genesis 17:5

Father God, in the name of Jesus Christ, give me a change of name in the order of Abraham that will depict my new status of relevance. Father God, in the name of Jesus, grant unto me a change of name that will reflect my purpose and assignment on earth.

2. Land Ownership

"And give thee the blessing of Abraham, to thee, and to thy seed with thee; that thou mayest inherit the land wherein thou art a stranger, which God gave unto Abraham."

Genesis 28:4

Father God, one of the outstanding blessings of Abraham that I crave and pray for is land ownership. Father, there is no award or reward for being landless or a tenant! Oh God I tap into these Abrahamic blessings today, give me landed properties in Jesus mighty name!

3.   Access to divine secrets

"And the LORD said, Shall I hide from Abraham that thing which I do; Seeing that Abraham shall surely become a great and mighty nation, and all the nations of the earth shall be blessed in him?"

Genesis 18:17-18

Father God, in the name of Jesus Christ, I place a demand for access to your secrets. Show me what lies ahead of me so that I can align my life with your plans and purpose.

4.   Blessing of Fruitfulness in old age

"For Sarah conceived, and bare Abraham a son in his old age, at the set time of which God had spoken to him."

Genesis 21:2

Father God, there is no barrier to Fruitfulness in old age, therefore I covet and pray for spiritual, mental and physical fruitfulness in the order of Abraham in Jesus mighty name!

5.   Blessed in all things

"And Abraham was old, and well stricken in age: and the LORD had blessed Abraham in all things."

Genesis 24:1

Father God, in the name of Jesus Christ, arise and bless me in all things like you did for Abraham.

6.   Blessing of Long life

"Then Abraham gave up the ghost, and died in a good old age, an old man, and full of years; and was gathered to his people."

Genesis 25:8

"And Abraham was an hundred years old, when his son Isaac was born unto him."

Genesis 21:5

Father God, in the name of Jesus Christ, I tap consciously into longevity of father Abraham today. In the name of Jesus, I receive the gift of long life. I shall only die in a good, ripe old age!

7.   Grace of Multiplication

"Remember Abraham, Isaac, and Israel, thy servants, to whom thou swarest by thine own self, and saidst unto them, I will multiply your seed as the stars of heaven, and all this land that I have spoken of will I give unto your seed, and they shall inherit it for ever."

Exodus 32:13

Father God, as Abraham's seed by faith in Jesus Christ, I pray for the grace of multiplication upon Abraham. By this grace, I shall not experience stagnated life. By this grace, I shall not be small or few in Jesus mighty name!

8.   Divine leading

"And I took your father Abraham from the other side of the flood, and led him throughout all the land of Canaan, and multiplied his seed, and gave him Isaac."

Joshua 24:3

Father God, in the name of Jesus Christ, I earnestly crave for your leadership. Father, just as you led Abraham throughout his sojourn in the land of Canaan, arise and lead me, and give me an inheritance in this land.

9.   Divine covenant

"Even of the covenant which he made with Abraham, and of his oath unto Isaac;"

1 Chronicles 16:16

"For when God made promise to Abraham, because he could swear by no greater, he sware by himself,"

Hebrews 6:13

Father God, just as you have ever been faithful to your promises and covenant to Abraham, may all your promises of blessings find practical fulfilment in my life in the name of Jesus Christ!

10.   Grace for Tithing

"To whom also Abraham gave a tenth part of all; first being by interpretation King of righteousness, and after that also King of Salem, which is, King of peace;"

Hebrews 7:2

Father God, in the name of Jesus, give me the grace for tithing in the footsteps of Abraham. Make me a template of a faithful tither. Help me not to rob you in my tithes and offerings in Jesus mighty name!

11.   Great blessings

"And he said, I am Abraham's servant. And the LORD hath blessed my master greatly; and he is become great: and he hath given him flocks, and herds, and silver, and gold, and menservants, and maidservants, and camels, and asses."

Gen 24:34-35

Father God, I want to be a template of great blessings in the order of father Abraham. I pray that you may enrich me greatly so that I may use my resources to serve you and your kingdom in Jesus mighty name!

12.   Eternity in the kingdom of heaven

"And I say unto you, That many shall come from the east and west, and shall sit down with Abraham, and Isaac, and Jacob, in the kingdom of heaven."

Matthew 8:11

Father God, I desire to spend eternity with father Abraham. Father, in the name of Jesus Christ, give me the grace to be among those that will sit down with Abraham in the kingdom of heaven!

#

Chapter Four

PRAYING FOR
MATERIAL BLESSINGS

"Therefore take no thought, saying, What shall we eat? or, What shall we drink? or, Wherewithal shall we be clothed? 32 (For after all these things do the Gentiles seek:) for your heavenly Father knoweth that ye have need of all these things. But seek ye first the kingdom of God, and his righteousness; and all these things shall be added unto you."

Matthew 6:31-33

God has never downplayed or downgraded material prosperity. In fact, He is quite aware of our material needs, and He is very much interested in meeting our material needs, just as He is, spiritually. Our Heavenly Father knows that we cannot survive in this material world without material resources, hence His desire and readiness to bless us materially.

The truth is that God is interested in putting food on your table! He is interested in giving you beautiful shelter! He wants you to be well clothed!

Without food, drink, and shelter you cannot maintain a safe and secure life. Hence, His readiness to provide for you. God does not want us to chase after material blessings like gentiles. His desire is that we pant after Him and His kingdom, and all these blessings shall be added unto us.

The honest truth is that if we mind or seek His kingdom, we may not have to be praying for material blessings!

Covet these blessings and pray thus:

1.   Finest of wheat

"He maketh peace in thy borders, and filleth thee with the finest of the wheat."

Ps 147:14

Father God, in the name of Jesus Christ, as I serve you and your kingdom, arise and fill me with the finest of wheat.

2.   Abundant blessings

"The thief cometh not, but for to steal, and to kill, and to destroy: I am come that they might have life, and that they might have it more abundantly."

John 10:10

Father God, arise and pour out your blessings on me more abundantly. May I be a reflection of your generosity as far as your material blessings are concerned in Jesus name.

3.   Power to enjoy material blessings

"Every man also to whom God hath given riches and wealth, and hath given him power to eat thereof, and to take his portion, and to rejoice in his labour; this is the gift of God."

Eccl 5:19

Father God, grant unto me the grace to enjoy all the material blessings you have graciously blessed me with.

4.   A curse into a blessing

"Nevertheless the LORD thy God would not hearken unto Balaam; but the LORD thy God turned the curse into a blessing unto thee, because the LORD thy God loved thee."

Deuteronomy 23:5

Father God, in the name of Jesus Christ, as I seek you and your kingdom passionately, arise and cause me to enjoy a reversal of fortune, from curses to blessings. Change my material poverty to material prosperity oh God, my Father!

5.   Restoration of material blessings

"And I will restore to you the years that the locust hath eaten, the cankerworm, and the caterpiller, and the palmerworm, my great army which I sent among you."

Joel 2:25

Father God, arise and make up to me for the years that the swarming locust has eaten.

6.   Divine supplies

"And my God shall supply all your need according to His riches in glory by Christ Jesus."

Philippians 4:19

Father God, in the name of Jesus Christ, arise and supernaturally supply my material needs today according to your riches in glory!

7.   Prosperity in all things

"Beloved, I pray that you may prosper in all things and be in health, just as your soul prospers."

3 John 2

Father, prosperity in all things is my portion! In the name of Jesus Christ, cause me to prosper materially even as I prosper spiritually. Father, cause me to enjoy sound health always!

8. Food and clothing

"Therefore I say unto you, Take no thought for your life, what ye shall eat, or what ye shall drink; nor yet for your body, what ye shall put on. Is not the life more than meat, and the body than raiment? Behold the fowls of the air: for they sow not, neither do they reap, nor gather into barns; yet your heavenly Father feedeth them. Are ye not much better than they?"

Matthew 6:25-26

Father God, by your grace and enablement, I shall no longer worry about what to eat, drink and clothe forthwith. If you can feed the birds of the air, you shall do much more for me, as I am of more value than them.

9. Power for wealth

"And you shall remember the Lord your God, for it is He who gives you power to get wealth, that He may establish His covenant which He swore to your fathers, as it is this day."

Deuteronomy 8:18

Father God, arise and empower me to command great wealth in Jesus mighty name!

10.   Prayer against Locust

"He gave also their increase unto the caterpiller, and their labour unto the Locust."

Psalms 78:46

Father God on the account of your mercy and favour do not give my material wealth to the Locust in Jesus mighty name!

Chapter Five
PRAYING FOR
FINANCIAL BLESSINGS

Financial blessings are real! God is still in the business of blessing His children financially. If today you have a financial blessing that you didn't have yesterday, then you're better off than you were yesterday. Financial blessings make you richer than before. When God blesses you financially, there is no Jupiter that can thwart your financial rest. It is His blessings that make you grow in wealth or riches. It is His blessings that cause you to grow from glory to glory financially. The Bible says, the path of the just is like the shinning light that shines more and more. You are meant to gather wealth progressively.

You know, some brethren get some financial blessings today, and they will be broke tomorrow. Some even had millions of Naira last year and this year there is no trace of a million. What a tragedy! The financial blessings which the

Lord provides are such that they never decrease. They always increase such that you are always richer today than you were the day before.

Why do we need financial blessings?

We need financial blessings because money is a defence! We need financial blessings because "money answereth all things." Money is needed to buy things! The Bible says, *"Men shall buy fields for money, and subscribe evidences, and seal them, and take witnesses in the land of Benjamin..."*

Jeremiah 32:44

Money is needed to pay taxes and other bills.

"And when they were come to Capernaum, they that received tribute money came to Peter, and said, Doth not your master pay tribute?"

Matthew 17:24

It is a blessing to move from poverty to prosperity!

It is a blessing to be free from debts!

It is a blessing to experience financial blessings

Praying for financial blessings is not enough!

There is what to do in order to move from financial frustration to financial rest. There is what to do to change your financial story.

- Become a diligent worker!
- Become a committed giver!
- Become a faithful tither, as your faithfulness in tithing is your surest way to commanding financial blessings. Please take this instruction: Give a financial sacrifice and tie whatever you want God to do for you to the offering!

- Believe Him for something great. Be rest assured that He will open strange doors of financial blessings for you. I read a story about a brother who sowed the only property he had which was a television set. That same year God gave him a vision to start a private school which is booming with so many students today.

My God will deliver you and your entire family from the grips of poverty. By the blood of Jesus, I secure your freedom from the dungeon of poverty. I bless you in the name of Jesus Christ with business ideas that will cause the establishment of mega business conglomerates.

PRAYERS:

1.   Great gifts of silver and gold

Father God, if an earthly father could give great gifts of silver and gold, you will do much more. In the name of Jesus Christ, arise and shower on me financial blessings forthwith.

"And their father gave them great gifts of silver, and of gold, and of precious things, with fenced cities in Judah: but the kingdom gave he to Jehoram; because he was the firstborn."

2 Chronicles 21:3

2.   Grace to sow financial seeds

Father God give me the grace and courage to sow financial seeds that will change my story. Father God help me to apply every word that will transform me from financial obscurity to the limelight.

"Be not deceived; God is not mocked: for whatsoever a man soweth, that shall he also reap."

Galatians 6:7

3.   Financial Favour

Father God, in the name of Jesus Christ, arise and cause me to be satisfied with financial favour and to be full with the blessing of the LORD in the order of Naphtali.

Empower me to possess the west and the south of my country.

"And of Naphtali he said, O Naphtali, satisfied with favour, and full with the blessing of the LORD: possess thou the west and the south."

Deuteronomy 33:23

4.   Access to Secrets

Father God, in the name of Jesus Christ, grant unto me access to your secrets that will help me to command financial blessings. Father God, you have promised to pour out water upon him that is thirsty, Lord I'm thirsty to locate secrets for financial blessings.

"The secret things belong unto the LORD our God: but those things which are revealed belong unto us and to our children for ever, that we may do all the words of this law."

Deuteronomy 29:29

5.   Wealth and riches

Father God, in the name of Jesus Christ, arise and fill my house with your blessings of wealth and riches forthwith.

"Wealth and riches shall be in his house: and his righteousness endureth for ever."

Psalms 112:3

6.   Bless the work of my hands

Father God, in the name of Jesus Christ, bless the work of my hands, so that I may experience financial increase. Oh Lord, establish my business to become an institution of reference.

"Hast not thou made an hedge about him, and about his house, and about all that he hath on every side? thou hast blessed the work of his hands, and his substance is increased in the land."

Job 1:10

7.   Grace to be a lender and not a borrower

Father God, in the name of Jesus Christ, I receive grace to be a lender and not a borrower.

"The rich ruleth over the poor, and the borrower is servant to the lender."

Proverbs 22:7

8.   The due season blessings

Father God, in the name of Jesus Christ, I decree that my business/work of my hands may yield her fruit in due season forthwith.

"And he shall be like a tree planted by the rivers of water, that bringeth forth his fruit in his season; his leaf also shall not wither; and whatsoever he doeth shall prosper."

Psalms 1:3

9. Feast of fat blessings

Father God, arise and make unto me a feast of fat things financially. May I enjoy the abundance of both material and financial blessings beyond measure in Jesus mighty name.

"And in this mountain shall the LORD of hosts make unto all people a feast of fat things, a feast of wines on the lees, of fat things full of marrow, of wines on the lees well refined."

Isaiah 25:6

10. Financial Rehoboth

Father God, in the name of Jesus Christ, arise and bless me in the order of Isaac. By faith I receive my financial Rehoboth. Make room for me so that no Philistine will contend or strive with me forthwith.

"And he removed from thence, and digged another well; and for that they strove not: and he called the name of it Rehoboth; and he said, For now the LORD hath made room for us, and we shall be fruitful in the land."

Genesis 26:22

Chapter Six

PRAYING FOR
SUNDRY BLESSINGS

There are other types of blessings that will interest you. In this chapter, I have decided to put together many other things you can pray about, such as:

1. Blessing of conception

Father God, in your power you caused a virgin to conceive and bring forth a son, arise and cause me to conceive and bring forth my own children in Jesus mighty name!

"And, behold, thou shalt conceive in thy womb, and bring forth a son, and shalt call his name JESUS."

Luke 1:31

Father God, you have promised to make the barren woman a joyful mother of children, arise in the name of Jesus Christ and bless me to become a joyful mother indeed.

"He maketh the barren woman to keep house, and to be a joyful mother of children. Praise ye the LORD."

Ps 113:9

2.   Blessings of children

Father God, in the name of Jesus Christ arise and cause my wife to become a fruitful vine, bearing Godly children that will serve you in their generation.

"Thy wife shall be as a fruitful vine by the sides of thine house: thy children like olive plants round about thy table."

Psalms 128:3

3.   Marital blessings

"Whoso findeth a wife findeth a good thing, and obtaineth favour of the LORD."

Proverbs 18:22

Singles pray thus:

Father God in the name of Jesus Christ, let my potential spouse locate and find me forthwith. Father, remove every veil that has kept him/her from seeing me.

Married couple pray thus: Father God, I thank you because my wife is a good thing that has happened to me. May I enjoy only good, not evil.

Father God, in the name of Jesus Christ, may the favour attached to marriage institution become our portion. May my spouse and I live to enjoy all kinds of blessings you have packaged in marriage institution forthwith.

4.   Earthly blessings

Father God, thank you for giving us the earth as humans. Lord God, I ask for the earthly blessings so that I can fulfil my destiny on earth, as it takes earthly blessings to be relevant on earth.

"The heaven, even the heavens, are the LORD'S: but the earth hath he given to the children of men."

Ps 115:16

Father God, may the earth yield her increase abundantly unto me even as I praise you always.

"Let the people praise thee, O God; let all the people praise thee. Then shall the earth yield her increase; and God, even our own God, shall bless us."

Psalm 67:5-6

5.   Blessings of business breakthroughs

Father God in the name of Jesus Christ, arise and cause my business to break forth on the right and on the lift. May my business experience breakthroughs, expansion and enlargement always so that I will become an envy to all my competitors.

"For thou shalt break forth on the right hand and on the left..."

Isaiah 54:3

6.   Blessings of promotion and elevation

Father God, you remain the lifter of man any day any time, in the name of Jesus Christ, arise and elevate me to the position where I will serve your purpose in my generation.

"For promotion cometh neither from the east, nor from the west, nor from the south. But God is the judge: he putteth down one, and setteth up another."

Psalms 75:6-7

7. Blessings of growth and Enlargement

Father God, in the name of Jesus Christ, let me experience growth and enlargement in my life.

Oh God arise and increase me more and more.

"And Jabez called on the God of Israel, saying, Oh that thou wouldest bless me indeed, and enlarge my coast, and that thine hand might be with me, and that thou wouldest keep me from evil, that it may not grieve me! And God granted him that which he requested."

1 Chronicles 4:10

8. Blessings of good treasure

Father God in the name of Jesus Christ open unto me your good treasure! Let the heavens release the rain of blessings upon me and my household. Father God enrich me greatly to become a lender and not a borrower.

"The LORD shall open unto thee his good treasure, the heaven to give the rain unto thy land in his season, and to bless all the work of thine hand: and thou shalt lend unto many nations, and thou shalt not borrow."

Deuteronomy 28:12

9.   Blessings of 100% Annual return

Father God, in the name of Jesus Christ, let every investment I make command a 100% return in the order of Isaac.

"Then Isaac sowed in that land, and received in the same year an hundredfold: and the LORD blessed him."

Genesis 26:12

10.   Blessings of children

Father God, in the name of Jesus Christ, arise and bless me with children in the order of Asher.

"And of Asher he said, Let Asher be blessed with children; let him be acceptable to his brethren, and let him dip his foot in oil."

Deuteronomy 33:24

11.   Blessings of inheritance

Father God, in the name of Jesus Christ, arise and bless me with great inheritance in the order of Caleb.

"And Joshua blessed him, and gave unto Caleb the son of Jephunneh Hebron for an inheritance."

Joshua 14:13

12.   Blessed Above others

Father God, in the name of Jesus Christ, arise and bless me above others in the order of Jael!

"Blessed above women shall Jael the wife of Heber the Kenite be, blessed shall she be above women in the tent."

Judges 5:24

13.   Blessings of abundance

Father God, in the name of Jesus Christ, arise and bless me with great abundance of resources.

"And Azariah the chief priest of the house of Zadok answered him, and said, Since the people began to bring the offerings into the house of the LORD, we have had enough to eat, and have left plenty: for the LORD hath blessed his people; and that which is left is this great store."

2 Chronicles 31:10

14.   Blessings of Excellence

Father God in the name of Jesus Christ arise and bless me with an excellent spirit in the order of Daniel.

"Then this Daniel was preferred above the presidents and princes, because an excellent spirit was in him; and the king thought to set him over the whole realm."

Daniel 6:3

Chapter Seven
PRAYING FOR FAVOUR

P rayer is a major key that unlocks every door that the enemy has shot against you! Has the door of favour been shot against you, your family or business? With prayers you can unlock the door, and provoke favour from God. John Wesley said that God does things for us in response to our prayers. We are expected to engage in   result-oriented prayers. According to E. M Bounds, "Prayer introduced those who practiced it into a world of privilege and brought the strength and wealth of heaven down to the aid of finite man." Let me also add here that with prayers you and I can procure or pull down from heaven divine favours for our earthly benefits and enjoyment.

Favour from God and man is one of the blessings indeed. As far as I'm concerned, the special favour from God remains a veritable force to make you change levels. It is a "blessing indeed" to experience a change of status. To move from an ordinary life to an extraordinary life will require God's intervention. And divine intervention is about God stepping into your life to make a worthwhile difference.

As a believer, do you want to be blessed indeed?

You sure need God's favour! You cannot amount to anything without His favour. Do you realise how some people labour vigorously every day of their life without tangible dividends or rewards? Do you know that there are people out there who find it difficult to make it in life, no matter their efforts?

One day of favour is superior to one thousand days of labour! God's favour will distinguish you, and you shall not suffer like others. These days, our world is faced with one crisis or the other. But the secret or key to our survival in these perilous times is God's favour. When you and I are shielded with His favour, no economic meltdown will affect us. No calamity will befall us! No evil will come near our dwelling! God shall isolate and envelope us from all evil machinations of the enemy. *"For thou, LORD, wilt bless the righteous; with favour wilt thou compass him as with a shield."*

Psalm 5:12

Do you want to take full delivery of your favour-inheritance in God? If yes, then accept personal responsibility to call upon God sincerely for favour. The

Bible says, *"I intreated thy favour with my whole heart: be merciful unto me according to thy word."*

Psalms 119:58

You can't call upon God in distress and be abandoned! He will set you free, and also set you in a large place where you will enjoy the benefits of His favour. In this place, no man can harm or do you evil, instead you will see your desire upon those that hate you. The Bible says, *"I called upon the LORD in distress: the LORD answered me, and set me in a large place. The LORD is on my side; I will not fear: what can man do unto me? The LORD taketh my part with them that help me: therefore shall I see my desire upon them that hate me."*

Psalm 118:5-7

The Bible says, *"Call unto me, and I will answer thee, and shew thee great and mighty things, which thou knowest not."*

Jeremiah 33:3

God has great and mighty favour-blessings, but you must call on Him in prayers to procure them into your life. Prayer is the instrument you need to provoke Heaven's attention! Nehemiah called on God in prayers for mercy, *"O Lord, I beseech thee, let now thine ear be attentive to the prayer of thy servant, and to the prayer of thy servants, who desire to fear thy name: and prosper, I pray thee, thy servant this day, and grant him mercy in the sight of this man. For I was the king's cupbearer."*

Nehemiah 1:11

Without Nehemiah's prayer for mercy or favour, he would not have been favoured by the king. Divine favour procured all the provisions and permission which he enjoyed from the king.

PRAYERS

1.   Favour as a shield

Father God, in the name of Jesus Christ, bless me and surround me with favour as with a shield.

"For thou, LORD, wilt bless the righteous; with favour wilt thou compass him as with a shield."

Psalms 5:12

2.   Favour from superiors

Father God, in the name of Jesus Christ, arise and grant unto me special favour in the sight of my superiors.

"But the LORD was with Joseph, and shewed him mercy, and gave him favour in the sight of the keeper of the prison."

Genesis 39:21

"And the king loved Esther above all the women, and she obtained grace and favour in his sight more than all the virgins; so that he set

the royal crown upon her head, and made her queen instead of Vashti."

Esther 2:17

"Now God had brought Daniel into favour and tender love with the prince of the eunuchs."

Daniel 1:9

3.   Favour in the sight of enemies

Oh God, arise and grant unto me favour in the sight of my enemies in Jesus mighty name!

"And I will give this people favour in the sight of the Egyptians: and it shall come to pass, that, when ye go, ye shall not go empty:"

Exodus 3:21

4.   Favour satisfaction

Father God, in the name of Jesus Christ, arise and satisfy me with favour in the order of Naphtali. Cause me, oh Lord, to possess precious things, gifts and properties in choice areas on the account of your favour in Jesus mighty name!

"And of Naphtali he said, O Naphtali, satisfied with favour, and full with the blessing of the LORD: possess thou the west and the south."

Deuteronomy 33:23

5.   Growth in favour with God and man

Oh God, my Heavenly Father, in the name of Jesus Christ, cause me to grow in favour with you and men in the order of Samuel.

"And the child Samuel grew on, and was in favour both with the LORD, and also with men."

1 Samuel 2:26

6.   Favour for preservation

Father God, in the name of Jesus Christ, grant unto me life and favour. Father, arise and preserve my soul from death.

"Thou hast granted me life and favour, and thy visitation hath preserved my spirit."

Job 10:12

7.   Evidence of favour

Father God, in the name of Jesus Christ, I thank you for not allowing my enemies to triumph over me. I know that to be protected and preserved is an evidence of your favour. For this, I give you all the glory.

"By this I know that thou favourest me, because mine enemy doth not triumph over me."

Psalms 41:11

8.   Set time of favour

Father God, because this is my set time to be favoured, in the name of Jesus Christ, arise and decorate my life with favour forthwith.

"Thou shalt arise, and have mercy upon Zion: for the time to favour her, yea, the set time, is come."

Psalms 102:13

9.   Special favour for your people

Father God, in the name of Jesus Christ, arise and cause me to be a partaker of your special favour which you have reserved for your people.

"Remember me, O LORD, with the favour that thou bearest unto thy people: O visit me with thy salvation;"

Psalms 106:4

10.   Good understanding for favour

Father God, in the name of Jesus Christ, arise and impart me with the Spirit of understanding. Give me special understanding that will procure special favour from you and man.

"Good understanding giveth favour: but the way of transgressors is hard."

Proverbs 13:15

Chapter Eight

PRAYING FOR SOCIAL BLESSINGS

The truth is that many believers are bereft of blessings because they lack social skills. Many find it extremely difficult to connect, walk or work with other people. They are not people friendly. Their inability to relate well or get along with others in church or in the society has robbed them of great blessings. What a shame!

It is a good and pleasant thing for believers to dwell and work together in unity. The Bible says,

"Behold, how good and how pleasant it is for brethren to dwell together in unity! It is like the precious ointment upon the head, that ran down upon the beard, even Aaron's beard: that went down to the skirts of his garments; As the dew of Hermon, and as the dew that descended upon the mountains of Zion: for there the LORD commanded the blessing, even life for evermore."

Ps 133:1-3

In this passage, I can eminently deduce that the Lord releases special blessings upon us when we dwell or relate with one another in unity. If my deduction holds sway, then it is germane that every believer should possess social skills, I mean the ability to relate well with people. You don't have to be a PR guru or expert to relate well with people! Believers must learn how to live and work with people within the sphere of their influence, so that they may enjoy the blessings packaged for them in the atmosphere of unity.

Can you live in this world without people? No! Whether you like it or not, you will find yourself working with other people, hence the importance of social skills. Believers who work as a team have the capacity to accomplish more than those who work individually. They accomplish more because they complement one another. They give strength to one another. They produce results far beyond the ordinary when they join their spiritual and material resources together in order to achieve the common objective of affecting the church of Jesus Christ positively.

Yes, we have a common objective to join hands with Jesus Christ to build and take His church to the next level. Do you want to command or achieve outstanding results for the Lord? If yes, then you sure need to work with others. Watchman Nee says, *"Alone I cannot serve the Lord effectively. . ."*

The Bible says, *"He that walketh with wise men shall be wise: but a companion of fools shall be destroyed."* (Proverbs 13:20).

There is a key principle in this passage: if you walk with wise men you shall be wise; if you also socialise with blessed people, you shall be blessed with blessings. May God give you the wisdom to know who to relate with to procure blessings indeed. Amen!

PRAYERS

1.   Concept of "Let us"

Father God, in the name of Jesus Christ, grant unto me the grace to embrace the concept of "Let Us" in my dealings with other people.

"And God said, Let us make man in our image, after our likeness: and let them have dominion over the fish of the sea, and over the fowl of the air, and over the cattle, and over all the earth, and over every creeping thing that creepeth upon the earth."

Genesis 1:26

"And they said, Go to, let us build us a city and a tower, whose top may reach unto heaven; and let us make us a name, lest we be scattered abroad upon the face of the whole earth."

Genesis 11:4

2.   Love one another

Father God, you are the God of love, grant unto me the grace to obey your commandment of love. Father, enable me in the name of Jesus Christ to love others always.

"This is my commandment, That ye love one another, as I have loved you."

John 15:12

"But as touching brotherly love ye need not that I write unto you: for ye yourselves are taught of God to love one another."

1 Thessalonians 4:9

3.   Preferring one another

Father God, in the name of Jesus Christ, arise and cause me to be kindly affectioned to others and to also prefer other people above myself.

"Be kindly affectioned one to another with brotherly love; in honour preferring one another;"

Romans 12:10

4.   Serve one another

Father God, arise and grant unto me the grace to use my liberty to serve others in Jesus mighty name!

"For, brethren, ye have been called unto liberty; only use not liberty for an occasion to the flesh, but by love serve one another."

Galatians 5:13

5.   Forbearing one another

Father God, in the name of Jesus Christ, arise and empower me with the spirit of meekness and patience to bear with others in love.

"With all lowliness and meekness, with longsuffering, forbearing one another in love;"

Ephesians 4:2

6.   Forgiving one another

Father God, it takes grace to forgive, in the name of Jesus Christ, arise and empower me with grace to always forgive those people who hurt or offend me.

"Forbearing one another, and forgiving one another, if any man have a quarrel against any: even as Christ forgave you, so also do ye."

Colossians 3:13

7.   Comfort and edify one another

Father God, in the name of Jesus Christ, let the Comforter release unto me the spirit of comfort so that I can effortlessly comfort and edify people within my sphere of influence.

"Wherefore comfort yourselves together, and edify one another, even as also ye do."

1 Thessalonians 5:11

8. Exhort one another

Father God, in the name of Jesus Christ, arise and empower me with the grace to always exhort the brethren daily.

"But exhort one another daily, while it is called To day; lest any of you be hardened through the deceitfulness of sin."

Hebrews 3:13

9. Finding solutions to common problems

Father God, grant unto me the grace to work with others to find solutions to common problems or challenges.

"And they said every one to his fellow, Come, and let us cast lots, that we may know for whose cause this evil is upon us. So they cast lots, and the lot fell upon Jonah."

Jonah 1:7

10.   Follow Peace with all men

Father God, in the name of Jesus Christ, arise and help me with grace to maintain peace with all people that I come across in my daily interactions.

"Follow peace with all men, and holiness, without which no man shall see the Lord:"

Hebrews 12:14

Chapter Nine
PRAYING FOR
HEALTH AND HEALING

I t is the blessing of the Lord to be in health always! It is the blessing of the Lord to be healed when you are sick. God's wish for you and I is that we might experience health 24/7!

The sick cannot be useful, as he or she is incapacitated due to ill health.

Health is superior to healing!

The benefits of health cannot be overemphasised!

PRAYERS:

1.   Take away Sickness

Father God, you promised to take away sickness from those that serve you. Arise and take away sickness from me and my family even as we serve you. Let my kingdom

Service procure health unto me always in Jesus mighty name.

"And ye shall serve the LORD your God, and he shall bless thy bread, and thy water; and I will take sickness away from the midst of thee."

Exodus 23:25

2.   Good Health

Father God, in the name of Jesus Christ, arise and bless me with good health always in the order of Jacob.

"And they answered, Thy servant our father is in good health, he is yet alive. And they bowed down their heads, and made obeisance."

Genesis 43:28

3.   Pleasant Words

Father God, in the name of Jesus Christ, may your word be pleasant to me, and causing me to gain health always. And may my words be pleasant to my hearers and provoking health to them.

"Pleasant words are as an honeycomb, sweet to the soul, and health to the bones."

Proverbs 16:24

4.   Restoration of Health

Father God, in the name of Jesus Christ, arise and restore my health, and heal all my wounds both physical and emotional forthwith.

"For I will restore health unto thee, and I will heal thee of thy wounds, saith the LORD; because they called thee an Outcast, saying, This is Zion, whom no man seeketh after."

Jeremiah 30:17

5.   Good Diets

Father God, in the name of Jesus Christ, arise and satisfy me and my family with good and healthy food. Let our diets be such that could provoke health instead of illness.

"Wherefore I pray you to take some meat: for this is for your health: for there shall not an hair fall from the head of any of you."

Acts 27:34

6.   Prosperity and Health

Father God, your paramount wish is that I should be in constant health, as such, arise and establish me in prosperity and health forthwith in Jesus mighty name!

"Beloved, I wish above all things that thou mayest prosper and be in health, even as thy soul prospereth."

3 John 1:2

7.   Miracle of Healing

Father God, in the name of Jesus Christ, arise and bless me and my family with the miracle of healing, such that no sickness or diseases will hold sway in our lives.

"For the man was above forty years old, on whom this miracle of healing was shewed."

Acts 4:22

8.   Gifts of Healing

Father God, in the name of Jesus Christ, bless me with the gifts of healing. Appoint me, oh God, as one of your agents designated for the healing of those that are oppressed with sickness.

"To another faith by the same Spirit; to another the gifts of healing by the same Spirit;"

1 Corinthians 12:9

9.   Power to Heal

Lord Jesus, by the power of the Holy Spirit, ordain me in the order of the Apostles and empower me to heal sicknesses and to cast out demons forthwith.

"And he ordained twelve, that they should be with him, and that he might send them forth to preach, And to have power to heal sicknesses, and to cast out devils:"

Mark 3:14-15

10.   Healing by His Stripes

Father God, in the name of Jesus Christ, I claim my healing by the stripes of Jesus. No sickness or disease shall have dominion over my soul and body anymore!

"Who his own self bare our sins in his own body on the tree, that we, being dead to sins, should live unto righteousness: by whose stripes ye were healed."

1 Peter 2:24

Chapter Ten

PRAYING AGAINST
SATANIC FORCES

"But while men slept, his enemy came and sowed tares among the wheat, and went his way."

Matthew 13:25

The honest truth is that satanic forces remain the greatest threat to your blessings! The enemy is the reason you are not enjoying some blessings. The devil is the enemy who has been sowing evil tares among your blessings. You must arise ferociously to resist him and his cohorts by all means! You've got the power, as Jesus Christ has given you the authority to tread on him and his cohorts. And nothing shall by any means hurt you or your destined blessings. The Bible says, *"Behold, I give unto you power to tread on serpents and scorpions, and over all the power of the enemy: and nothing shall by any means hurt you."*

Luke 10:19

The devil and his agents have the ministry to pervert the right ways of God! If you allow him, he will pervert your business, marriage or anything that gives you joy and peace. The Bible says, *"... O full of all subtilty and all mischief, thou child of the devil, thou enemy of all righteousness, wilt thou not cease to pervert the right ways of the Lord?"*

Acts 13:10

The devil throws party when you fail! He wants you to remain on the floor permanently. Micah said, *"Rejoice not against me, O mine enemy: when I fall, I shall arise; when I sit in darkness, the LORD shall be a light unto me."*

Micah 7:8

PRAYERS:

1.   No to every evil Harassment

Father God, in the name of Jesus Christ, I say no to every evil harassment forthwith. Father God, arise and give me rest on every side, so that no enemy will be able to harass me any more.

"But now the LORD my God hath given me rest on every side, so that there is neither adversary nor evil occurrent."

1 Kings 5:4

2.   Contend with my contenders

Father God, in the name of Jesus Christ, arise and contend with those that contend with me. All that war against my life and blessings shall be as nothing and as a thing of nought forthwith.

"Thou shalt seek them, and shalt not find them, even them that contended with thee: they that war against thee shall be as nothing, and as a thing of nought."

Isaiah 41:12

3.   Household Enemies

Father God, in the name of Jesus Christ, I come against every household enemy standing against my blessings and my general well-being.

"And a man's foes shall be they of his own household."

Matthew 10:36

4.   Permanent Shame and Reproach

Father God, in the name of Jesus Christ, arise and give me a token of your blessings so that those that hate me may be put into permanent shame and reproach.

"Shew me a token for good; that they which hate me may see it, and be ashamed: because thou, LORD, hast holpen me, and comforted me."

Psalms 86:17

5. An Enemy to my enemies

Father God, in the name of Jesus Christ, arise and become an enemy to my enemies, and become an adversary to my adversaries forthwith.

"But if thou shalt indeed obey his voice, and do all that I speak; then I will be an enemy unto thine enemies, and an adversary unto thine adversaries."

Exodus 23:22

6. Deliverance from the hand of the enemy

Father God, in the name of Jesus Christ, arise and deliver me and my family from the hand of my enemies forthwith

"Or, Deliver me from the enemy's hand? or, Redeem me from the hand of the mighty?"

Job 6:23

7. Deliverance from strong enemies

Father God, in the name of Jesus Christ, arise and deliver me from my strong enemy that is against my promotion, breakthrough and enlargement.

"He delivered me from my strong enemy, and from them which hated me: for they were too strong for me."

Psalms 18:17

8.   Great Triumph

Father God, the evidence that you are blessing or favouring me is that you will never allow my enemy to triumph over me. Father God, in the name of Jesus Christ, arise and give me great triumph over my enemies forthwith.

"By this I know that thou favourest me, because mine enemy doth not triumph over me."

Psalms 41:11

9.   Deliverance from indebtedness

Father God, in the name of Jesus Christ, deliver me miraculously from every enemy of indebtedness. Empower me financially to pay up my debts.

"Then she came and told the man of God. And he said, Go, sell the oil, and pay thy debt, and live thou and thy children of the rest."

2 Kings 4:7

10.   No weapon against me

Father God, by the blood of Jesus, I pray against every evil plan or agenda targeting my blessings.

I decree that every evil plan of the devil against my desire to excel in life be frustrated and defeated. No weapon formed/fashioned against me shall prosper in Jesus name!

*"**No weapon that is formed against** thee shall prosper; and every tongue that shall rise against thee in judgment thou shalt condemn. This is the heritage of the servants of the LORD, and their righteousness is of me, saith the LORD."*

Isaiah 54:17

Epilogue
PRAYING FOR
OTHER PEOPLE

Dear reader, I must not fail to show you one vital key which I consider so paramount in your quest to connecting or obtaining divine blessings. This key is praying for other people! The honest truth is that, your preponderance of not praying for others is the height of selfishness. To be bombarding the gate of heaven every now and then just to satisfy your own needs is nothing but self-aggrandisement.

I want you to do a review of your prayers lately. You may discover that you lack consideration for others in your prayers. Check out your prayer requests for the past one week or one month, you will be ashamed of yourself that all you are telling God is about yourself. Prayer is not all about "give me, give me!" You must create a Prayer-space for your friends, relatives, business partners, professional colleagues, or even your enemies. Jesus said, *"But I say unto you, Love your enemies, bless them that curse you, do good to them that hate you, and pray for them which despitefully use you, and persecute you."*

83

Matthew 5:44

You must be prepared and willing to intercede for other people, especially those close to you. Intercession involves taking hold of God's will and refusing to let go until His will comes to pass in the lives of people you are interceding or praying for.

It is the will of God for all men to be saved. Pray for the salvation of all men! It is the will of God for your loved ones to experience prosperous journey or journey mercies. Pray for them whenever they are embarking on any journey! The Bible says, *"Making request, if by any means now at length I might have a prosperous journey by the will of God to come unto you."*

Romans 1:10

It is the will of God for you and others to be sanctified. Pray for the sanctification of your loved ones and the church of God. *"For this is the will of God, even your sanctification, that ye should abstain from fornication:"*

1 Thessalonians 4:3

Intercessory prayer is a serious matter! If you can pray seriously for others as you normally do for yourself, God will shower His blessings on you as never before!

Beloved reader, it is to your own advantage to pray for other people! There are many people around you that have needs of blessings like you.

Tell me who is not interested in being blessed!

Tell me who's not happy if he or she is blessed! Every one wants to be blessed. Praying for someone to be blessed is your sure way to be blessed faster. Until Job prayed for his friends he himself was not blessed. But it was when he prayed for his friends that God turned his captivity. The Bible says, *"... the LORD turned the captivity of Job, when he prayed for his friends: also the LORD gave Job twice as much as he had before."*

Do you want your captivity to be turned? Then locate a friend who is passing through some challenges or problems and pray vehemently for that person. You will be surprised at how God will turn your own capacity.

God loves people! He loves it when you stand in the gap for others. Actually, God is in dire need of intercessors, men and women that will call upon Him on behalf of others. God is looking for prayer warriors that will pray less for themselves but pray much for others and the land. The Bible says, *"And I sought for a man among them, that should make up the hedge, and stand in the gap before me for the land, that I should not destroy it: but I found none."*

Ezekiel 22:30

Your prayers could keep someone alive tonight.

The Bible says, *"And all the people said unto Samuel, Pray for thy servants unto the LORD thy God, that we die not..."*

1 Samuel 12:19

Until you and I come to the point in our Christian walk, where we view our failure to praying for others as an ungodly act, we will not take this intercession-assignment seriously. Every true or sincere intercessor should know that it is a sin not to pray for others. Samuel was a great intercessor. He felt he would be sinning if he failed to pray for the people of Israel. *"Moreover as for me, God forbid that I should sin against the LORD in ceasing to pray for you: but I will teach you the good and the right way:"*

1 Samuel 12:23

5 Great Intercessors

1.   Jesus Christ

"Therefore will I divide him a portion with the great, and he shall divide the spoil with the strong; because he hath poured out his soul unto death: and he was numbered with the transgressors; and he bare the sin of many, and made intercession for the transgressors."

Isaiah 53:12

"Wherefore he is able also to save them to the uttermost that come unto God by him, seeing he ever liveth to make intercession for them."

Hebrews 7:25

2. The Holy Spirit

"Likewise the Spirit also helpeth our infirmities: for we know not what we should pray for as we ought: but the Spirit itself maketh intercession for us with groanings which cannot be uttered. And he that searcheth the hearts knoweth what is the mind of the Spirit, because he maketh intercession for the saints according to the will of God."

Romans 8:26-27

3. Prophets

"But if they be prophets, and if the word of the LORD be with them, let them now make intercession to the LORD of hosts, that the vessels which are left in the house of the LORD, and in the house of the king of Judah, and at Jerusalem, go not to Babylon."
Jeremiah 27:18

4. Apostles

"For this cause we also, since the day we heard it, do not cease to pray for you, and to desire that ye might be filled with the knowledge of his will in all wisdom and spiritual understanding;"

Colossians 1:9

5.   Christian Brethren

"Brethren, pray for us."

1 Thessalonians 5:25

"Finally, brethren, pray for us, that the word of the Lord may have free course, and be glorified, even as it is with you:"

2 Thessalonians 3:1

Who should we pray for?

1.   Kings, Leaders and those in authority

"That they may offer sacrifices of sweet savours unto the God of heaven, and pray for the life of the king, and of his sons."

Ezra 6:10

"I exhort therefore, that, first of all, supplications, prayers, intercessions, and giving of thanks, be made for all men; 2 For kings, and for all that are in authority; that we may lead a quiet and peaceable life in all godliness and honesty. 3 For this is good and acceptable in the sight of God our Saviour."

1 Tim 2:1-3

2. Apostles (Church leadership)

"Finally, brethren, pray for us, that the word of the Lord may have free course, and be glorified, even as it is with you:"

2 Thessalonians 3:1

3. Friends

"And the LORD turned the captivity of Job, when he prayed for his friends: also the LORD gave Job twice as much as he had before."

Job 42:10

4. Disciples (Christians)

"I pray for them: I pray not for the world, but for them which thou hast given me; for they are thine."

John 17:9

5. All men

"I exhort therefore, that, first of all, supplications, prayers, intercessions, and giving of thanks, be made for all men;"

1 Tim 2:1

If you are struggling or stagnated in life, do consult me for counselling and prayers.

joejesimiel2006@yahoo.com

Facebook: Joe Jesimiel Ogbe

Other Books
by the Author

1.   Teenagers and Relationships

2.   The Youth God Uses

3.   Building an Effective youth ministry

4.   Can Boys and Girls also go to Hell?

5.   Securing your Marital Destiny

6.   Questions that Singles Ask

7.   How to Obtain Favour from God and Man

8.   Pathways to a Blissful Courtship

9.   Becoming Rich and Wealthy

10.   Strategies for a stress-free Relationship

11.   Enjoying God's Mercy

12.   Getting what you want by Faith

13.   Hebrew Women's Style (Divine Tips for mothers to be)

14.   Pathways to Academic Success

15.   Youth and Friendship

16. Youth and Opportunity